THE HISTORY OF EXPLORATION

AFRICA

NEW
FOREST
PRESS

WHAT IS AFRICA?

Africa has always held a strong fascination for those living outside of its shores. For people of the past, Africa represented mystery, adventure, and even danger. Yet as more of Africa was opened up, that sense of wonder only increased. The explorers returned with tales that were as fantastic as the myths that had previously surrounded this continent. Africa today remains a land of huge contrasts. To talk about something being "African" is difficult because of all the differences that exist within its boundaries—in particular, its people and the land on which they live. It is thanks to the explorers of Africa that these wonders were first revealed to the rest of the world.

THE WILDLIFE OF AFRICA

Africa has a huge number of animal species. Its rain forests contain primates such as gorillas, monkeys, and chimpanzees. The savannas of eastern and southern Africa have large herds of wildebeests (gnu), elephants, and zebras. The inland waters are home to the hippopotamus, crocodile, and huge flocks of birds.

LIVING ON THE EDGES OF AFRICA

The diversity of Africa's population increased with the arrival of new immigrants who originally came from Europe, South Asia, and Arabia, like this Tunisian shepherd boy.

MOUNT KILIMANJARO

Mount Kilimanjaro in Tanzania is Africa's highest mountain, rising to 19,336 ft. (5,895m). The first Europeans to reach Mount Kilimanjaro were two Germans, Johannes Rebmann and Ludwig Krapf, whose tales of a snow-covered mountain near the equator were not believed at first.

AFRICAN COUNTRIES

There are 54 countries in Africa. They vary widely in size and population. There are more than 149 million Nigerians, and yet the tiny state of São Tomé and Príncipe has only around 213,000 people.

Nile

Sahara Desert

Atlas Mountains

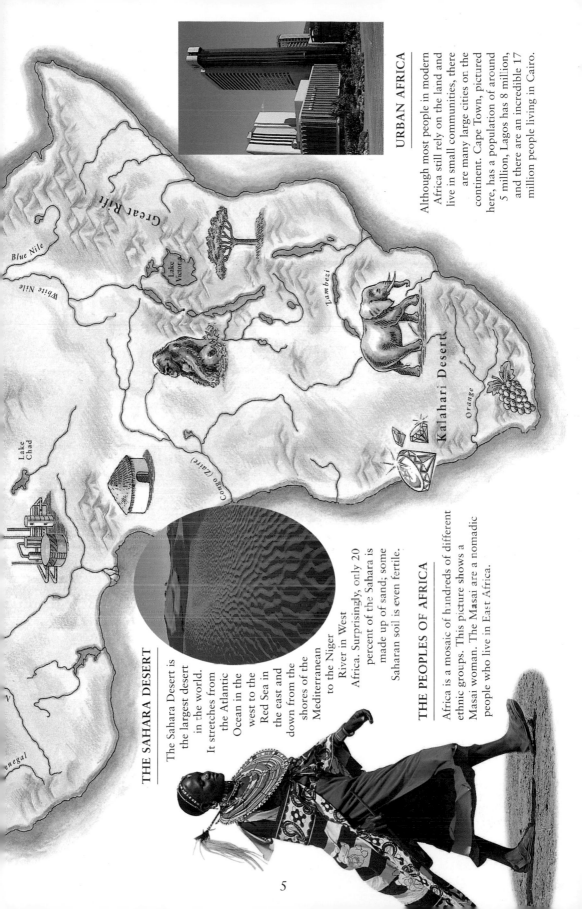

Although most people in modern Africa still rely on the land and live in small communities, there are many large cities on the continent. Cape Town, pictured here, has a population of around 5 million, Lagos has 8 million, and there are an incredible 17 million people living in Cairo.

Great Rift

Blue Nile

White Nile

Lake Victoria

Zambezi

Lake Chad

Kalahari Desert

Congo (Zaire)

Orange

Senegal

THE SAHARA DESERT

The Sahara Desert is the largest desert in the world. It stretches from the Atlantic Ocean in the west to the Red Sea in the east and down from the shores of the Mediterranean to the Niger River in West Africa. Surprisingly, only 20 percent of the Sahara is made up of sand; some Saharan soil is even fertile.

THE PEOPLES OF AFRICA

Africa is a mosaic of hundreds of different ethnic groups. This picture shows a Masai woman. The Masai are a nomadic people who live in East Africa.

5

EARLY EXPLORERS OF AFRICA

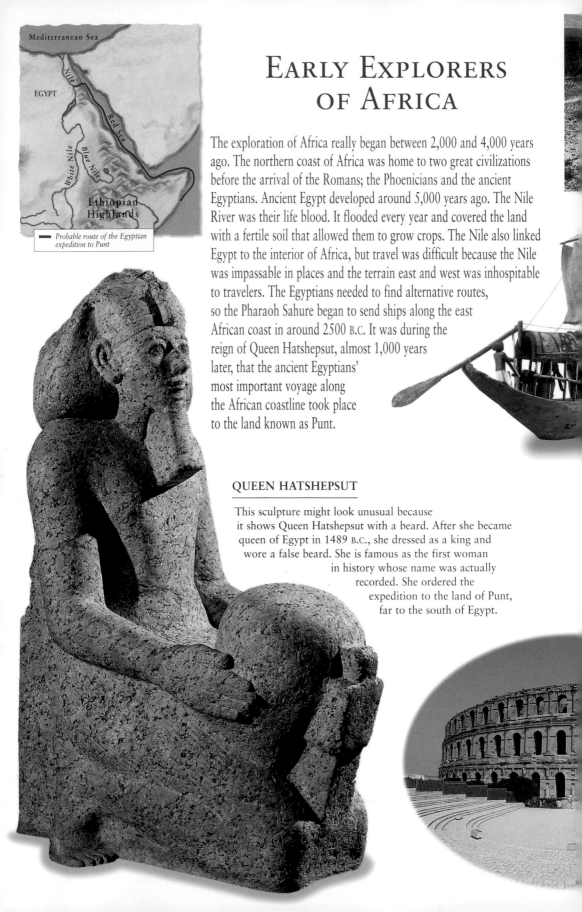

Probable route of the Egyptian expedition to Punt

The exploration of Africa really began between 2,000 and 4,000 years ago. The northern coast of Africa was home to two great civilizations before the arrival of the Romans; the Phoenicians and the ancient Egyptians. Ancient Egypt developed around 5,000 years ago. The Nile River was their life blood. It flooded every year and covered the land with a fertile soil that allowed them to grow crops. The Nile also linked Egypt to the interior of Africa, but travel was difficult because the Nile was impassable in places and the terrain east and west was inhospitable to travelers. The Egyptians needed to find alternative routes, so the Pharaoh Sahure began to send ships along the east African coast in around 2500 B.C. It was during the reign of Queen Hatshepsut, almost 1,000 years later, that the ancient Egyptians' most important voyage along the African coastline took place to the land known as Punt.

QUEEN HATSHEPSUT

This sculpture might look unusual because it shows Queen Hatshepsut with a beard. After she became queen of Egypt in 1489 B.C., she dressed as a king and wore a false beard. She is famous as the first woman in history whose name was actually recorded. She ordered the expedition to the land of Punt, far to the south of Egypt.

ARRIVAL AT PUNT

One of the reasons for the expedition to Punt was to bring back myrrh trees. Myrrh is used to produce incense, which was used in religious rituals. The location of Punt is not clear, but as myrrh trees only grew in the area around modern-day Ethiopia and Somalia, most people now believe that they landed in Somalia. They returned to Egypt laden with goods, not just with myrrh, but with ivory, ebony, and slaves.

SAILING THE RED SEA

Egyptian sailing boats were made by tying planks of wood together with rope. When rope gets wet, it shrinks and this meant that the planks were always held together tightly. For the voyage to Punt, the sails would have been made larger than usual so that they could use the south wind that blows down from the Mediterranean. Each ship was around 70 ft. (21m) long with a crew of 30. Five ships set off on the voyage down to the Red Sea. They may have sailed close to the coast, and the crew may have spent the night ashore, but some historians now believe that these ships were not capable of such a sea voyage and that they traveled down the Nile.

DEIR EL BAHRI

We know a lot about the Egyptians' expedition to Punt because Queen Hatshepsut had the story of the voyage carved on to the walls of her burial temple, built near Thebes at Deir el Bahri. Many objects made from the raw materials brought back from Punt were put into this temple. We do not know exactly when Queen Hatshepsut died.

THE ROMANS ARRIVE IN NORTH AFRICA

The great civilization of ancient Egypt began to decline in the years leading up to the birth of Christ. Much of northern Africa was conquered by the Romans by around 150 B.C., and Egypt came under their control in 30 B.C. This amphitheater in El Djem in Tunisia is the third-largest amphitheater in the Roman world. It was built in A.D. 230 and held 50,000 spectators. The Romans rarely explored the continent, but a Roman expedition is said to have reached the Tibesti highlands in modern Chad and Libya.

~c. 2500 B.C.~
The ancient Egyptian pharaoh Sahure begins an exploration of the east African coast

~1489–1469 B.C.~
Queen Hatshepsut is the ruler of Egypt and sends an expedition to the land of Punt in what is now believed to be Somalia

~c. 600 B.C.~
Greek historian Herodotus writes of a voyage by Phoenician sailors right around the African coast

~c. 425 B.C.~
The Phoenician admiral Hanno begins his great voyage along the east African coast

~c. 150 B.C.~
Romans complete their conquest of North Africa

~1349–1354~
Ibn Battuta travels through Muslim Africa

~1445~
The Portuguese sail around Cape Verde, the western tip of West Africa

~1482~
Diego Cão discovers the Congo River

~1485~
Leo Africanus is born

~1488~
The Cape of Good Hope is reached by Bartolomeu Diaz

~1497~
Vasco da Gama rounds the Cape of Good Hope and sails up the east African coast

SETTING OFF FROM CARTHAGE

These ruins are all that remain of the great city-state of Carthage. The most famous of the Phoenician voyages was made from here by the admiral Hanno around 425 B.C. He set sail with 60 ships; on board were hundreds of men and women. During the first part of the voyage, he founded six colonies along the Moroccan coast. Hanno then continued to sail south with just two ships. He probably sailed up part of the Senegal River and then continued as far as Nigeria before returning home.

THE GREATEST MUSLIM VOYAGER

In 1325, a young man from Tangier in Morocco set off for Mecca in Arabia. His name was Ibn Battuta. On the way to Mecca, he decided to travel over all of the known Muslim world, beginning a great journey that took him nearly 30 years. It is known that in this time he visited Spain, the Middle East, China, India, and Southeast Asia. He also explored the north of Africa, crossed the Sahara Desert to the Niger River in West Africa, and traveled as far as modern-day Tanzania on the east African coast.

SAILING ON A PHOENICIAN SHIP

The Phoenicians were excellent shipbuilders, building both warships (as on this coin) and a type of sailing ship known as a Hippoi. It had a single sail, two rows of oars on either side of the ship, and a pointed front that was used to ram enemy ships in battle. The ship was steered with two large oars at the back on either side.

A PAPAL COMMISSION

Until Europeans began to explore the interior of Africa in the 17090s, most of their ideas about Africa came from one source. It was a book called *The Description of Africa* by Leo Africanus, that was published in 1526. Leo Africanus was born in 1485 in Granada in what is now Spain but was then a Muslim state. In 1492, the Muslims were finally forced out of Spain, and he went to live in Morocco. He worked as a diplomat in North Africa and the kingdom of Ghana before he was captured by Christian pirates. He was given to Pope Leo X (left) as a slave. Leo freed him and commissioned him to write a detailed survey of Africa.

THE PHOENICIANS IN AFRICA

After the Egyptians, the next great explorers of Africa were the Phoenicians. These were a people who originally came from an area known as Canaan in modern-day Syria and Lebanon. They became great traders, and by 1100 B.C., they were the masters of the Mediterranean. They are known to have sailed to the Atlantic Ocean and visited England in 450 B.C. Their most important exports were timber, especially cedarwood, and a purple dye made from shellfish. The word "Phoenicia" comes from a Greek word meaning purple. In order to protect their trade, Phoenicians began to set up colonies in Spain, Sicily, Sardinia, and North Africa. Their most famous colony was the city of Carthage in modern-day Tunisia. With the decline of the Phoenician Empire, there are few accounts of further exploration of Africa until the arrival of the Portuguese in the 1400s.

A VOYAGE AROUND AFRICA?

According to the ancient Greek historian Herodotus, the Egyptian pharaoh Necho II hired a crew of Phoenicians in 600 B.C. to sail all of the way around the coast of Africa. Herodotus wrote that it took the crew three years to make the journey. Every spring, they landed and planted grain. Only after the grain had been harvested did they continue with their voyage. We do not know whether this story is true, as there is no other evidence.

The Portuguese in Africa

BUILDING FORTS ALONG THE COAST

The Portuguese were not interested in the interior of Africa. The whole continent was simply an obstacle on the way to the riches of Asia. However, they did build a series of fortified towns along the African coast to protect and supply their ships. The picture shows Fort Jesus in the Kenyan town of Mombasa.

In 1492, Christopher Columbus managed to convince the Spanish monarchs, Ferdinand and Isabella, to pay for a voyage across the Atlantic Ocean. He wanted a westward route to the riches of Asia, while Portugal was looking eastward. The Portuguese had been sailing along the coast of West Africa for some time. By 1419, they had reached Madeira, and in 1431, they discovered the Azores. In 1445, Portuguese ships had sailed around Cape Verde. By 1482, they crossed the equator and had gotten as far south as the mouth of the Congo River. When the Spanish discovered a "New World" to the west, it was believed that they had reached the Asian continent, rather than America. This made the Portuguese search for their own route around Africa more urgent.

MEETINGS ON THE AFRICAN COAST

As the Portuguese sailed down the western coast of Africa, they found that many of the peoples they met belonged to highly developed societies. This bronze model of a Portuguese soldier was made by a member of the Benin Empire. The people of Benin lived in what is now Nigeria.

PRINCE HENRY THE NAVIGATOR

Prince Henry directed the early Portuguese exploration of West Africa. He dreamed of launching a crusade to destroy Muslim North Africa. Finding a way to Asia would help pay for this crusade and at the same time would weaken the hold that the Muslims had over the trade in gold and spices between Europe and Asia.

MARKED WITH A CROSS

Among the supplies that Vasco da Gama carried on his voyage were stone crosses called padroes. These were set in high ground as markers for the sailors who were to follow them. They were also used to claim newly discovered lands. This cross is at Malindi in modern-day Kenya.

ARRIVAL IN INDIA

It took another ten years after Bartolomeu Diaz had discovered the route around Africa for the Portuguese to eventually sail all the way to Asia. Vasco da Gama set off from Portugal in July 1497, and guided by an East African pilot across the Indian Ocean, he finally arrived at the southern Indian port of Calicut in May 1498.

THE LEGEND OF PRESTER JOHN

The main reason why Europeans were searching for a seaward route to Asia was because the land route was controlled by hostile Muslims. There was a legend of a Christian king named Prester John who ruled over an African kingdom just beyond Muslim North Africa. Portuguese explorers hoped to find Prester John and join with him to fight the Muslims.

AFRICA
-A TIMELINE-

~1526~
The Description of
Africa *by Leo Africanus
is first published*

~1768~
*James Bruce, the Laird
of Kinnaird, begins
his voyage across
Egypt and Ethiopia*

~1770~
*James Bruce reaches Lake
Tana in Ethiopia, which
he mistakenly believes
is the source of the
Nile River*

~1771~
Mungo Park born

~1795–1797~
*Mungo Park goes in
search of the source of
the Niger River*

~1813~
David Livingstone born

~1822~
*Hugh Clapperton crosses
the Sahara Desert to
Lake Chad*

~1824–1828~
*René Caillié travels
through West Africa
to Timbuktu*

SHIPS & SAILING

The crews of the early voyages of exploration faced many dangers. Not only did they have to put up with cramped conditions and only a small supply of food and water (which was often bad), but they were usually sailing into the unknown with little idea where they were and how fast they were traveling. Perhaps it is not surprising, therefore, that many early explorers had to face mutiny. Today, ships have little trouble locating their exact position. Accurate maps, clocks, and global positioning satellites (GPS) mean that sailors can tell where they are to within a few feet. Sailors hundreds of years ago were not so fortunate.

MAGNETIC COMPASS

It was vitally important that the sailors crossing the Ocean knew exactly in what direction they were sailing. On a clear day or night, either the Sun or the North Star were used. They could also use a magnetic compass. The magnetic field around Earth meant that a magnetized needle floating in water would always point northward.

DEAD RECKONING

If a navigator knew where his ship sailed from, what its speed was, the direction the ship was traveling in, and how long they had been traveling, then it was possible to calculate how far they had traveled by "dead-reckoning" and so find their position. However, winds and tides meant that this was only an approximate way of figuring out the ship's position. The early explorer Christopher Columbus was regarded as a great navigator because of his skill with "dead-reckoning."

THE ASTROLABE

One of the oldest altitude measuring devices is the Astrolabe. This is an Arabic example of an Astrolabe. It could be used to find out how far north or south of the equator (latitude) the ship was. It worked by measuring the height of the North Star or noon Sun from the ship. Once the height was known, then the navigator could calculate how far north or south he was. The first documented use of it used at sea is in 1481 on a voyage down the African coast by Portuguese explorers.

THE CROSS-STAFF

In the early days of exploration, the simplest way to measure the latitude of a ship was to use an instrument called a cross-staff. It had a crossbar for sighting and a rod with measurements cut into the side. The crossbar would be lined up between the Sun or North Star and the horizon. The measurements of the long piece of wood would then tell the navigator the angle of the Sun or star from the horizon. From this, he could figure out his latitude. There is considerable danger in staring at the Sun for too long. In 1595, Captain John Davis invented the backstaff, which used mirrors and shadows so that navigators did not risk being injured.

TELLING THE TIME

For early navigators to calculate a ship's position, it was vital that they knew what time of day it was. Sailors would be given the job of watching a large sand-filled hourglass (similar to the 17th-century example, shown here). It normally emptied after 30 minutes and then a bell would be rung so that everybody on board knew what the time was.

THE QUADRANT

Explorers also took quadrants with them on their voyages. The earliest documented use of the quadrant at sea is in the mid 1400s. Quadrants did basically the same job as astrolabes. They worked by lining up one arm with the horizon and then aligning a movable arm to point at either the Sun or Pole Star. The angle between these two arms could then be used to calculate the ship's latitude. It could only really work when the sea was calm and still.

FOLLOWING THE COAST

The Portuguese were not interested in exploring the interior of Africa. They did trade with the peoples they encountered, but they were looking for a sea route to the Indies. However, they knew that places on the coast of Africa were important landing stages for ships. The route round Africa to Asia took many years to discover. In 1482 King John II sent Diogo Cão to find the Indies. He did not find it but he did discover that Africa was much larger than many people thought. It was Bartolomeu Diaz in 1488 who finally sailed around the southern tip of Africa. He followed the coast of Africa and sailed further south than any other European had managed until then.

BARTOLOMEU DIAZ

Diaz's ships were driven out of sight of land by a fierce storm. When it became calm he sailed north and found that the coast was now on his left and not his right as expected. He had sailed around the southern tip of Africa by accident.

BUILDING IN AFRICA

The Portuguese did not explore the interior of Africa and they decided not to establish any African colonies at this stage. However, they knew they had to protect their trade routes to Asia so they built a series of forts along the coastline. They could supply and protect Portuguese ships and keep out foreign competitors.

TRADING WITH AFRICANS

The two things that the Portuguese wanted when trading with the Akan and Benin peoples were gold and slaves. The Akan supplied most of West Africa's gold, which came from rivers in the interior of Africa. The Portuguese bought this gold from the Akan with slaves they had either captured themselves or bought from the Benin people. Many slaves were also transported back to Portugal and sold again.

THE CAPE OF GOOD HOPE

When Bartolomeu Diaz reached the southern tip of Africa he decided to call it "Cabo Tormentoso," which means the Cape of Storms. King John II rejected this name because it was too gloomy and gave it the name Cape of Good Hope, because it raised hopes of eventually reaching the Indies.

The Search for the Source of the Nile

The search for the source of the Nile had fascinated people for centuries. Ancient Greeks and Romans used the expression "to seek the head of the Nile" when they were describing an impossible task. For a long time, it was believed that if the source could be found, then all the rest of the mysteries of the interior of Africa would be revealed. By the 1800s, the need to discover the source became more than just satisfying people's curiosity. The European powers were beginning to expand their influence around the world, and the Nile was recognized as an important part of that expansion.

SIR RICHARD BURTON

Sir Richard Francis Burton was an intrepid English explorer who traveled with John Hanning Speke in search of the source. Apart from discovering Lake Tanganika, he is also known for visiting the Muslim holy cities of Mecca and Medina in disguise.

SIR SAMUEL WHITE BAKER

With a complicated river like the Nile, there were bound to be mistaken claims by those who were looking for its origins. However, the expedition of Sir Samuel Baker did help determine where the Nile *didn't* start. In 1861, he followed the river south and discovered Lake Albert Nyanza on the border of the Congo and Uganda. He found that the Nile simply flowed through the lake.

MEETING OF THE NILE EXPLORERS

The picture shows Speke and Grant meeting up with Sir Samuel Baker in 1863. The other person at the table is Samuel Baker's wife, Florence. At a time when women were not expected to do anything even mildly adventurous, she traveled with her husband during all of his expeditions. She had married Samuel Baker after being bought by him at a slave market in Bulgaria.

ANCIENT VIEW OF THE NILE

This picture is known as Ptolemy's world map, though it was actually drawn in 1482, more than 1,000 years after his death. The Nile is shown coming from a series of lakes far to the south of the equator. Just below these lakes is a mountain range called the Mountains of the Moon.

FALLS ON THE BLUE NILE

The Nile is the longest river in the world, at more than 4,092 mi. (6,000km) long. There are several tributaries that also feed the main river. These include the Blue Nile, that starts in the highlands of Ethiopia, and the smaller tributaries in Burundi, Kenya, and Tanzania. Around 1,860 mi. (3,000km) of the Nile is navigable.

JAMES BRUCE

The Scottish aristocrat James Bruce, Laird of Kinnaird, set off in 1768 and traveled across Egypt and Ethiopia in search of the source of the Nile. In 1770, he reached Lake Tana in Ethiopia, which he mistakenly believed was the source. He had found the source of the Blue Nile, a tributary to the main river. He was not the first European to reach Lake Tana—a Spanish missionary had been there more than 150 years earlier.

THE SOURCE DISCOVERED

It was the British explorer John Hanning Speke who found the true source of the Nile. In 1856, Speke and Sir Richard Burton went to search for great lakes in East Africa. In 1858, they found Lake Tanganyika. Speke traveled on alone after Burton got sick and discovered Lake Victoria, which he believed was the source of the Nile. Lake Victoria lies within Uganda, Tanzania, and Kenya. He returned there with James Grant in 1862 and found the point at which the Nile flowed out of the lake.

MOUNT KENYA

Mount Kenya is an extinct volcano in central Kenya. It is 17,053 ft. (5,199m) high and is Africa's second-highest mountain. The summit was first reached in 1899 by a party led by the British geographer Sir Halford Mackinder.

AFRICA'S GREAT RIFT

The Ngorongoro Crater in Tanzania is just one of the remarkable features of Africa's Great Rift. A series of faults in Earth have created a region cutting from the Red Sea down to Mozambique that is made up of mountains, volcanoes, valleys, and deep lakes. A branch in the east is named after John Gregory, a British explorer and geologist who explored the region in 1893.

GUSTAV NACHTIGAL

Gustav Nachtigal was a German explorer who, in 1868, was sent by the king of Prussia on a mission to Kanem-Bornu, a powerful kingdom situated in the Lake Chad region. He was the first European to travel through areas of the central Sahara in what is now Chad and the Sudan. He arrived back in Cairo, Egypt in 1874.

EXPLORING EAST AFRICA

From the 600s onward, East Africa increasingly came under the influence of Arab traders from the Middle East. The Arabs built many towns and ports along the coast that were used as centers for trading and as a base for sending slaves back to Arabia. With the arrival of the Portuguese explorer Vasco da Gama in 1498, control of the east African coast gradually moved from the Arabs to the Europeans, especially after the Arab fleet was destroyed by the Portuguese at the Battle of Diu in 1509. Any country that wanted to dominate trade with Asia, especially India, had to be in control of the east African coast. By the end of the 1800s, this meant that the interior of East Africa was explored, mapped, and claimed on behalf of various European countries. As the power of Portugal declined, it was the British and the newly created countries of Germany and Italy that increasingly took control of East Africa.

LAKE TANGANYIKA

Lake Tanganyika is located along the Rift Valley. It is the second-largest lake in Africa and the second-deepest lake in the world. It is bounded by Tanzania, the Congo, Burundi, and Zambia. The first Europeans to reach Lake Tanganyika were John Hanning Speke and Sir Richard Burton in February 1858. At first, they thought that they had found the source of the Nile.

JOSEPH THOMSON

Joseph Thomson was a Scottish explorer who traveled over most of eastern and southern Africa. He studied geology at the University of Edinburgh before leading an expedition to lakes Tanganyika and Rukwa in 1879–1880. Four years later, he became the first European to cross modern-day Kenya.

AFRICA
-A TIMELINE-

~1830~
*Richard and John Lander
find the source of
the Niger*

~1835~
*The Boers begin the
Great Trek*

~1841~
Henry Stanley is born

~1848~
*Johannes Rebmann and
Ludwig Krapf discover
Mount Kilimanjaro*

~1849–1852 ~
*Livingstone's first exploration
of Africa's interior*

~1852–1856~
Livingstone's second voyage

~1855~
*Livingstone sees Victoria
Falls for the first time*

~1856~
*John Hanning Speke and
Sir Richard Burton begin
their search for the source
of the Nile*

~1858~
*Lake Tanganyika discovered
by Speke and Burton*

A ROMANTIC EXPLORER

René Caillié was inspired to explore Africa after reading Daniel Defoe's novel *Robinson Crusoe*. He took up a challenge from the French Geographical Society to reach Timbuktu and return with an account of his journey. Caillié started his journey in Sierra Leone, disguised himself as an Arab, and joined a trade caravan heading for Timbuktu. The fact that he could not speak Arabic and knew nothing of the Muslim faith remarkably aroused little suspicion. He eventually arrived home to a hero's welcome.

CONTACT WITH WEST AFRICANS

All of these explorers met a wide variety of different people in their travels. In West Africa, the main societies were the Mande and Akan groups who lived in Ghana and the Cote D'Ivoire (Ivory Coast). The Fulani, Hausa, and Yoruba peoples lived around what is now Nigeria. There are many other groups throughout all of West Africa. The Cote D'Ivoire, where this mask comes from, has more than 60 ethnic groups within its borders.

MUNGO PARK

Mungo Park was born in Scotland in 1771 and trained to be a surgeon. He led an expedition to the Niger River, and after landing in what is now the Gambia, he traveled inland, going farther eastward that any other European had been. He was captured by a local tribe and was a prisoner for four months before escaping. He reached the Niger in 1796 and only turned back when his supplies ran out. He returned nine years later to explore the Niger by canoe, but this time his expedition was attacked by local people and he was drowned.

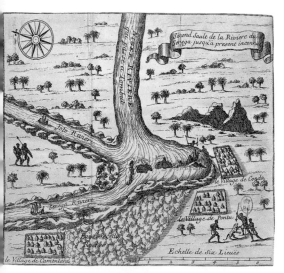

EXPLORING WEST AFRICA

Much of the West African coast was very well known to Europeans by the 1800s. It was due to the Portuguese explorers of the 1400s that this entire area had been thoroughly mapped and charted. Until the building of the Suez Canal in 1869, the only viable way for Europeans to reach Asia was by sailing around Africa. This meant that all of this part of the west coast was very important since whoever controlled it could have some control over the sea route to Asia. It was also from this part of Africa that Europeans took slaves to work on their plantations in the Caribbean and America. By the end of the 1800s, it was British and the French who controlled the coastline. Explorers of both countries began to travel into the interior of West Africa.

MEETING THE HAUSA

In 1822, the Scottish explorer Hugh Clapperton crossed the Sahara Desert to Lake Chad. He then went on to become the first European to come into contact with the Hausa people of northern Nigeria. After a short return home, he returned to find where the Niger River flowed into the sea. He died near Sokoto in April 1827 without achieving his goal.

FRANCE CLAIMS THE CONGO

The most famous French explorer of Africa, Pierre De Brazza was an Italian aristocrat by birth who took French citizenship. He explored West Africa for six years during the 1870s and 1880s. As the picture shows, De Brazza convinced many African leaders to accept French influence in the area.

FROM EAST TO WEST

The English explorer Verney Lovett Cameron was the first European to cross Africa from east to west. In 1873, he led an expedition to search for the explorer David Livingstone. Finding him dead, Cameron went on to the Zambezi and Congo rivers, and here he is being received by a king of the Congo region.

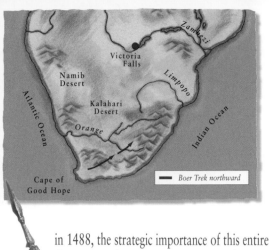

Namib Desert · Atlantic Ocean · Victoria Falls · Zambezi · Kalahari Desert · Orange · Limpopo · Indian Ocean · Cape of Good Hope

— Boer Trek northward

EXPLORING SOUTHERN AFRICA

Of all the parts of Africa that Europeans came into contact with, it was southern Africa where their presence was felt the most. From the moment Bartolomeu Diaz accidentally sailed around the Cape of Good Hope in 1488, the strategic importance of this entire region was instantly recognized by every seafaring European power. The Portuguese had not been interested in colonizing southern Africa, so it was the Dutch who were the first to settle there in the middle of the 1600s. They became known as Boers, which comes from the Dutch word for "farmer." By the 1800s, other European colonists began to arrive, especially from Great Britain. Tension began to arise between these different groups, and as a result, Boers moved farther into the unexplored areas of South Africa.

THE DUTCH EAST INDIA COMPANY

The Dutch East India Company was established to conduct Eastern trade and, in turn, created a Dutch empire in Southeast Asia in the 1600s and 1700s. It had control of all commerce between the Dutch Republic and the East.

A COLONY ON THE CAPE

The Dutch settled in Table Bay to grow vegetables for passing ships, to build a hospital for sailors, and to repair ships. Jan van Riebeeck's first fort was modern-day Cape Town's first building. It was to become the first town founded by Europeans in southern Africa.

THE DUTCH COLONY BEGINS

In 1652, the Dutch East India Company gave in to repeated petitions and recommendations from their ships' officers and decided to establish a post at Table Bay at the bottom of Table Mountain. They sent three small ships, the *Dromedaris*, the *Reijger*, and the *Goede Hoop* under the command of the 23-year-old Jan Antony van Riebeeck, a ship's surgeon, to establish a stronghold on the shores of Table Bay.

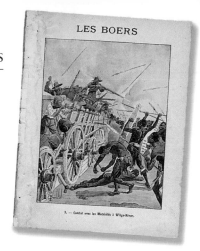

THE GREAT TREK

From 1835 until 1843, the Boers began an epic journey that became known as the Great Trek. More than 14,000 people left Cape Colony and moved inland to set up new colonies in Natal, the Orange Free State, and the Transvaal. The Great Trek took place for two reasons—the Boers were looking for new pastures for their cattle, and they were unhappy with British control of Cape Colony, especially after the British abolished slavery in 1833. During the Great Trek, the Boers came into conflict with native Africans, especially the Matabele and Zulus, who did not want these new arrivals on their land.

AFRICAN RESISTANCE

It was not only the Dutch who had to fight Africans before laying claim to African lands. In the 1870s, the Zulu chief Cetewayo asked the British authorities to protect his lands from the Boers. The British responded by invading Zululand in 1879. Cetewayo defeated the British in Isandhlwana before finally being crushed.

GREAT ZIMBABWE

As the Boers moved into new areas, they believed that they were settling in areas where no civilization had been before. The complex of ruins of Great Zimbabwe covers almost 2,000 acres. It is said to be built by Shona people in the 1200s or 1300s. It may have housed as many as 40,000. The first Europeans to see it were unwilling to believe that it was built by Africans because there was nothing else like it in all of southern Africa.

23

ARRIVING AT THE CAPE

Cape Colony had originally been colonized by the Boers like the ones shown in this picture. When Livingstone arrived in March 1841, it was under British control. He moved north and started his missionary work. By 1849, the urge to travel was too strong, and Livingstone joined an expedition to cross the Kalahari Desert. They became the first Europeans to reach Lake Ngami in modern-day Angola. When Livingstone returned to his home, he wrote to London announcing the news of their discoveries.

WORKING AT THE MILL

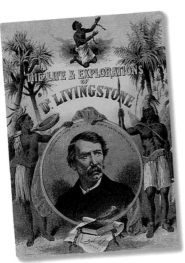

Livingstone started work at a cotton mill next to his house when he was ten years old. He read constantly and soon decided to become a doctor. In 1836, he managed to get to medical school in Glasgow, Scotland. While he was there, he became interested in the work of the London Missionary Society and decided to do missionary work in China. The Society accepted Livingstone but sent him to southern Africa instead.

GROWING UP IN GLASGOW

David Livingstone was born in 1813 and was raised on the edge of Glasgow, Scotland. He shared a single room with his parents, two brothers, and two sisters. The room was around 48 sq. ft. (4.5 sq. m). Although this seems small now, at the time it was regarded as being quite comfortable.

FROM SOLDIER TO JOURNALIST

In 1862, Henry Stanley joined the army. He soon found himself fighting in the American Civil War (1861–1865) on the side of the Confederates, who were later to lose the war. Stanley was wounded in his first battle and taken prisoner. After he recovered, he became a sailor and later a journalist. He worked for the *New York Herald* in Europe and Africa, and in 1871, he was sent to find Livingstone.

STANLEY & LIVINGSTONE

There have been many great pairs of explorers: including Burke and Wills in Australia and Lewis and Clark in America. In Africa, the famous pairing was Richard Burton and John Speke, who found the true source of the Nile. Yet the most famous pair of explorers of all must be David Livingstone and Henry Stanley, despite the fact that they met only once and spent just a few months together. Between them, they opened up more of Africa to the outside world than anybody else, but their reasons for being in Africa could not have been more different. Livingstone was there to spread the Christian gospel and to help put an end to slavery. Stanley arrived on the continent as a journalist seeking the greatest story of his career.

WHO WAS HENRY STANLEY?

Henry Stanley's real name was John Rowlands. He was born in Wales in 1841, the year that Livingstone arrived in Africa. His mother was an unmarried teenager who did not want him. He lived with his father and then moved into a workhouse, where he received a basic education. When he was 15, he sailed from Liverpool, England to New Orleans, where he started work in a store owned by a man named Henry Stanley.

LIVINGSTONE'S FAMILY JOINS AN EXPEDITION

This picture shows Livingstone on another expedition in 1851 to explore the rivers around Lake Ngami. He took with him his pregnant wife and their three children. In the picture Livingstone is holding the hand of his son Robert. In August, he arrived at the mighty Zambezi River. He decided to explore it more, and when his family returned to Great Britain in June 1852, he embarked on his greatest expedition yet.

THE SECOND EXPEDITION

When Livingstone set off on his second expedition in June 1852, he had little idea that he would not see his family for four years. He did not know that he would travel more than 5,600 mi. (9,000km) through parts of Africa that had never been seen by any European. On this expedition he explored more of the Zambezi River and was the first white person ever to see the Victoria Falls. When he returned to Great Britain, he was a national hero and easily found the money for his next two expeditions in 1858 and 1866. During this last expedition, Livingstone was away for so long that most people in Great Britain assumed that he was dead. *The New York Herald* sent Stanley to discover if this was true, and their meeting is now one of the most famous in history. After five months, Stanley returned to Europe to tell an expectant public of his adventures. Livingstone remained in Africa and died there in May 1873.

THE DEATH OF LIVINGSTONE

When Stanley left Livingstone in March 1872, he left behind a sick and weak man. But Livingstone continued with his travels for another eight months until he died on May 1, 1873. His African companions, including his servant Chuma, (*above*), preserved his body and carried it more than 1,240 mi. (2,000km) to the coast. Livingstone was buried in Westminster Abbey and mourned as a national hero.

VICTORIA FALLS

For three years, from 1852 to 1855, Livingstone had been following the Zambezi River downstream. Frequent illness and low supplies often slowed down the expedition. However, on November 16, 1855, Livingstone saw the Victoria Falls. The local name for the Falls was "Mosi-oa-Tunya," which meant "smoke that thunders." Livingstone decided to rename it after the British queen, Victoria.

FIGHTING THE SLAVE TRADE

One of the main reasons that Livingstone returned to Africa was to fight the slave trade. His determination to rid Africa of this evil was strengthened in July 1871, when he witnessed a massacre of more than 400 Africans by Arab slave traders. It was Stanley who brought back news of this massacre, and the strength of public opinion forced the British government to take action against the slave traders. Ironically, Stanley became notorious for treating his African porters harshly. He put them in chains to stop them from running away, and many died accompanying him.

STANLEY AND LIVINGSTONE MEET

Led by an African carrying the American flag, Stanley traveled more than 500 mi. (800km) inland from the east African coast. As Stanley approached Ujiji on the shores of Lake Tanganyika, he was told that a white man was staying there. Stanley changed into his cleanest clothes and walked into Ujiji. He stepped up to Livingstone and said, "Doctor Livingstone, I presume?"

Essential Equipment for African Explorers

Whenever any European explorer arrived in Africa, they were stepping into the unknown. Explorers had to travel across the variety of landscapes that make up Africa. They could find themselves in a seemingly empty desert, a foul-smelling swamp, or a thick rain forest. Even with African guides, they did not know what dangers and obstacles they would have to face. To overcome these problems, and since these expeditions sometimes took several years, explorers had to take several tons of equipment. Carrying all of this, and sharing the dangers, were native porters.

CARRYING A GUN

Two of the dangers that were faced by explorers were attacks either by wildlife or by native people who thought that they might be slave traders. Therefore, a gun was a useful tool for both dangers. Stanley often made use of the elephant gun that he is carrying in this picture. The explosive bullet was powerful enough to destroy a small boat. Although most animals kept away from teams of explorers, Livingstone himself was once attacked by a lion.

USING A COMPASS AND SEXTANT

Since much of the exploration of the interior of Africa was done by river, it may not be surprising that explorers used the same type of navigational equipment used by sailors. This compass and sextant were used by Livingstone during his travels along the Zambezi River. The compass was used to discover the direction in which the explorers were going. The sextant measured the angles between two stars and the horizon to establish their longitude.

THE MENACE OF THE MOSQUITO

The greatest menace faced by any African explorer was the often fatal disease of malaria, which in 1888 was discovered to be transmitted by mosquito bites. However, the explorers did know that quinine could help prevent malaria, and many of them took some on their expeditions.

CARRYING THE EQUIPMENT

When traveling by land, explorers depended on African porters to carry their equipment. Neither Livingstone nor Stanley traveled with less than 20 African porters, and most explorers had more than 50. These men and women would carry loads of around 110 lbs. (50kg) each day.

EXPLORERS CLOTHING

European explorers did not even dream of wearing the same clothes as their African porters, and many of them wore clothes that were similar to what they might wear at home. One exception was the pith helmet, which was developed by the British army in India. It was made from compressed plant fibers and had a deep brim. Some helmets had ventilation holes that helped keep the head cool.

CROSSING WATERFALLS

When explorers came up against barriers such as rapids and waterfalls, they had no choice but to carry the boat around the obstacle. This picture shows porters carrying dug-out canoes alongside the Congo River.

AFRICA
-A TIMELINE-

~1858~

Speke finds Lake Victoria, the source of the Nile

~1858–1864~

Livingstone explores the Zambezi River

~1860–1863~

Speke returns to Lake Victoria with James Grant

~1861~

Sir Samuel and Florence Baker follow the Nile south and discover Lake Albert Nyanza

~1866–1873~

Livingstone's last voyage

~1868–1874~

Gustav Nachtigal becomes the first European to travel through the central Sahara Desert

~1873~

David Livingstone dies

~1873–1875~

Verney Lovett Cameron is the first European to cross Africa from east to west

~1874–1877~

Henry Stanley explores the Congo River

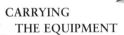

CARL THUNBERG

It was because of two men that the wonders of Africa's living world were brought to international attention. They were the Swedes Carl Thunberg (pictured here) and Anders Sparrman. In 1722, they traveled to the Cape of Good Hope. On arrival, they headed for the Table Mountain and in the space of one day managed to collect more than 300 plant specimens, many of which they had never seen before.

PROVIDING MEDICINE

Because they had lived in Africa for thousands of years, many Africans had developed a natural resistance to diseases such as malaria. However, this resistance did not offer complete protection, and there were many other diseases such as yellow fever or cholera. The ability to immunize against some of these diseases by vaccination was a practice started in England in 1796. This picture shows European doctors giving vaccinations to African children. Stanley made sure that all of his porters were given quinine, which helps protect against malaria.

ANIMALS AS TROPHIES

Hunting has always been a central feature in the lives of many Africans. It was essential for survival, and even the first European settlers hunted for food. The Boers were responsible for the extinction of the quagga, a type of zebra. For later settlers, hunting for food was less important than hunting for sport. The most popular hunting areas in the 1800s were Kenya in East Africa and Zambia in southern Africa.

DRAWING THE WILDLIFE

Today, most people hunt African animals with cameras rather than guns, but in the 1900s, cameras were rare and naturalists could only shoot or draw the animals that they saw. Many of the naturalists who came to Africa, such as William Paterson or Cornwallis Harris, were also talented artists. Their drawings and watercolors beautifully capture the colorful variety of Africa's natural world.

SCIENCE & RECREATION

The flora and fauna of Africa remained a mystery to western people for centuries. It was believed that the bones of lions were as hard as flint and created sparks when they were struck together. It was said that a rhinoceros killed its prey by knocking it down and licking it to death. Elephants always stirred the water with their trunks before drinking because they could not bear to see their own reflections. Yet, as with so much of Africa, the truth managed to be even more unusual than these stories. Naturalists and scientists who came to Africa were amazed by the variety of wildlife that they encountered, and they hurried to take specimens home. William Burchell, an English naturalist, returned from South Africa with thousands of specimens, including 265 bird skins and more than 120 animal skins. There were other Europeans who were interested in the animals of Africa. They were not scientists but hunters who entertained themselves by shooting the wildlife. Unfortunately their enthusiasm for their sport meant that some species were rapidly driven to the point of extinction. Today many African animals are protected by international laws preventing their slaughter.

PLANT HUNTING

Many of the naturalists who came to Africa discovered rare and beautiful plants. Cape Colony in South Africa was a treasure trove for all botanists. There were plants that attracted insects by smelling of rotting flesh, and others that flowered only at night. The picture (above) shows the extraordinary Protea, the national flower of South Africa.

A WOMAN IN AFRICA

At a time when women were not expected to look much farther than their homes, Africa lured in some exceptional female explorers. Perhaps the most famous is Mary Kingsley, who, interested in new species of animals, explored most of West Africa. She lived with native people there and in 1894 was the first European to visit parts of Gabon.

31

SPREADING THE WORD

In several European countries and in North America, missionary societies were formed in order to try and convert Africans to Christianity. David Livingstone was sent to Africa by the London Missionary Society. Most of these societies worked with little money, and they had to rely on missionaries who traveled around in tents.

A SCOTTISH MISSIONARY

One of the best-known missionaries in Africa was Robert Moffat. He was sent to South Africa by the London Missionary Society in 1816, and he stayed for more than 50 years. He encouraged Livingstone to explore Africa, and later Livingstone married Moffat's daughter, Mary.

RELIGION & ECONOMICS

Many of the Europeans who followed in the footsteps of the explorers were not interested in discovering new lands and new peoples. In the 1800s, it was sincerely believed that the European or American way of life was superior to anything else that existed at that time. When some Europeans looked at Africa, they saw a continent that appeared to be empty of agriculture and industry. Others were concerned with changing the people of Africa who they saw as primitive and superstitious, and if these people could be converted to Christianity then Africa would become more "civilized." Many Europeans came to Africa in order to develop this undeveloped continent. Some of these new arrivals saw opportunities for themselves, but all felt it necessary to impose their ways and beliefs on those that they regarded as inferior.

LOOKING FOR PRECIOUS STONES

In February 1867, a 15-year-old Boer named Erasmus Jacobs found a shining stone on the bank of the Orange River. It was a diamond. Within 15 years, South Africa was producing more diamonds than any other part of the world.

INTRODUCING CROPS

European farmers began to introduce crops that were more profitable than native plants into Africa. Many of these new plants, such as the peanut, sweet potato, or the cocoa bean as shown left, originally came from the Americas. These crops are still important to many modern African countries.

BUILDING AN AFRICAN CHURCH

Today, there are around 380 million Christians in Africa. They are roughly divided between the Roman Catholic Church and the various Protestant churches. Africa is home to the largest church in the world. The Basilica of Our Lady of Peace in Yamoussoukro in the Cote D'Ivoire was completed in 1989. It has a total area of 1,054,863 sq. ft. (98,000 sq. m) and can seat 7,000.

THE CHALLENGE OF ISLAM

The Islamic faith had already made many converts in Africa. When Islam spread across North Africa in the 600s and 700s, it also spread southward to those areas that bordered the Sahara Desert. The east African coast had been dominated by Arab traders for centuries, and the Muslim faith was very strongly rooted.

INTRODUCING AGRICULTURE

For centuries, Africans practiced a form of agriculture called slash-and-burn. A small area of forest was cut down and burned. The land was farmed until the fertile soil was used up and then abandoned before being gradually reclaimed by the forest. This method of farming began to vanish with the introduction of European farming methods.

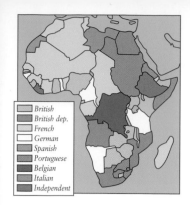

THE CARVING UP OF AFRICA

19th-century Europe was changing fast. Nations that once depended on agriculture for their wealth now relied on industry and manufacturing. In order to grow more prosperous, Europeans searched for new ways to sell more of their produce and to find cheap raw materials to make their goods. Explorers had shown that the interior of Africa was, more than likely, rich in resources to be exploited. The European countries made sure that they could control the African market by taking over large areas of the continent. During the 1800s, Europe saw the creation of three new states, Belgium, Italy, and Germany. These three countries looked to Africa as a way of proving that they were equal to any of the older nations such as France and Great Britain. As Africa was "carved up" by these European powers, nobody stopped to wonder what the people of Africa actually wanted for themselves.

AFRICA DIVIDED

This map shows how the European nations divided up Africa between them. Belgium kept the Congo. France had most of West Africa. Britain had a large share, including most of southern Africa. Germany, Portugal, and Spain also took chunks of land. By the end of the 1800s there were only two independent African nations, Liberia and Abyssinia, which is now Ethiopia.

THE BERLIN CONFERENCE

King Leopold's actions in the Congo prompted other European powers to lay claim to much of the rest of Africa. Sometimes these claims were a source of argument between the various nations. In 1884, a conference of European nations was held in Berlin to sort out these disputes, and Africa was formally divided. In this picture, an African looks on helplessly as his destiny is decided by European leaders.

AFRICAN RESISTANCE

Many Africans did not want their lands to be ruled by Europeans, and resistance was widespread. However, they could do little against heavily armed and disciplined armies, and hundreds of thousands of Africans died. One of the most formidable opponents the British had to face were the Zulus, who were eventually defeated in 1879.

RHODES: THE EMPIRE BUILDER

Cecil John Rhodes was a British politician who did more than anybody to bring southern Africa under British rule. In 1890, he became Prime Minister of Cape Colony and used his power to weaken the power of the Boers. As the picture shows, he dreamed of creating an empire from the Cape to Cairo. He invaded the lands of the Shona and Ndebebe people in what was later called Rhodesia before its name was changed again to Zimbabwe.

KING LEOPOLD OF BELGIUM

Leopold II hired Henry Stanley to carve out an empire for him in Central Africa, which he called the Congo Free State. He claimed it was to advance the cause of the abolition of slavery. By the 1880s, it was clear that Leopold's real motive was to develop a rubber industry there and that Belgians were themselves acting cruelly toward the Africans in the Congo.

AFRICA -A TIMELINE-

~1879~
The Zulu king, Cetewayo, is defeated by British forces

~1879–1880~
Joseph Thomson explores lakes Tanganyika and Rukwa

~1883–1884~
Joseph Thomson becomes the first European to cross modern-day Kenya

~1884~
The Berlin Conference is held

~1887–1889~
Stanley's last expedition to Africa

~1893~
Mary Kingsley explores parts of the Congo

~1894–1895~
Modern-day Gabon is explored by Mary Kingsley

~1899~
Mount Kenya is successfully climbed by Sir Halford Mackinder

~1904~
Stanley dies

THE BOER WAR

When gold was discovered in South Africa in 1884, thousands of British settlers came to make their fortune. Resentment between these newcomers and the Boers eventually turned into conflict, and in 1899, the Boers declared war on Great Britain. It took three years for the British army to eventually defeat them.

35

AFRICA & INDEPENDENCE

A SYMBOL OF PRIDE

In 1965, the white rulers of Rhodesia declared themselves independent of Britain rather than allowing democracy. African resistance to this was led by Robert Mugabe and Joshua Nkomo. In March 1980, additional international pressure forced the Rhodesian government to hold elections. Mugabe's ZANU-PF party won, and Rhodesia became Zimbabwe.

In February 1960, the British Prime Minister, Harold Macmillan gave a speech to the South African parliament in Cape Town. He spoke of a new African nationalism that was sweeping through the continent. He said, "the wind of change is blowing through this continent and . . . this growth of national consciousness is a political fact." Those winds had started blowing after the end of World War II. The Allies had fought to allow European and Asian countries to choose their own governments. Africans began to ask why the same should be not true for them, and demands for self-rule became louder. Sometimes the Europeans handed over power without a struggle. Sometimes Africans had to fight for independence. Since the 1950s, every African country has managed to become independent. However, it was only in 1994, when South Africa became a democratic country, that the continent was returned to the people to whom it had originally belonged before the explorers came.

THE LAST OUTPOST

After World War II, the South African government passed a series of laws that made the black population second-class citizens in their own land. This system of government was called "apartheid." Black South Africans struggled against this injustice both peacefully and with weapons. In 1990, Nelson Mandela, the leader of the African National Congress, was released from prison after 27 years. In April 1994, the first multiracial elections were held, and Mandela, aged 75, became the president of a new South Africa.

THE FUTURE OF AFRICA

Africa has to face many of the same problems as the rest of the developing world. Every African government has the twin challenges of improving the living standards of their people while having to cope with a growing population and increasing environmental damage. The estimated population of Africa is 840 million, and by 2025, it is projected to be 1,228 million. This is mostly because almost half of all Africans alive today are, like these children in Nairobi, aged under 15.

CONFLICT IN AFRICA

Many of these newly independent countries had borders that had been created by the Berlin Conference. Different groups of people that had lived separately for centuries suddenly found that they now lived in the same country. This has been one of the main reasons for the civil wars that have become a way of life in several African countries today.

AFRICA WORKING TOGETHER

This picture shows Nelson Mandela being helped down from a platform by other African presidents, after addressing the Organization of African Unity in June 1998. The organization was founded in 1958 and exists to help African countries find common solutions to common problems.

THE FIRST INDEPENDENT

The first colony to become independent after the end of World War II was the Gold Coast in 1957. The name of the country was changed to Ghana soon after independence. Kwame Nkrumah became the first African leader of a new African country.

AFRICA TODAY

Africa is the second-largest continent in the world. The world's biggest desert, the Sahara, dominates the landscape of the north, while in the south, forests and huge grasslands are home to wild animals such as leopards, lions, and elephants. The Great Rift Valley, one of Earth's major geological features, runs from the Red Sea down to Mozambique. Africa is home to many different people who practice numerous religions and live highly varied lifestyles. Africa is also home to some of the poorest people in the world. Some Africans live with drought and famine. Other Africans in the south live with civil wars and political unrest. Many African countries have large international debts to pay. However, Africa has one important resource—the young people who want to build a new future for their continent.

CITY LIFE IN CAIRO

Life in Egypt's capital, Cairo, is a mixture of modern and ancient. Cars, taxis, and buses share the crowded streets with donkey carts. Many people make their living from the tourists who come to see the wonders of ancient Egypt. The lives of affluent Egyptian people are very similar to those of prosperous people in European cities. For poor people, life is not very different from the way it was hundreds of years ago. Cairo is the African city with the largest population—17 million people.

THE TUAREG PEOPLE

The nomadic Tuareg people live in the Sahara Desert and the dry grasslands south of the Sahara. The Tuareg territory covers parts of five African countries—Libya, Algeria, Mali, Niger, and Burkina Faso. In the past, the Tuareg traded across the desert on their camels and carried goods. Today, most goods are transported by truck. Tuareg move with their herds of camels, sheep, and goats to find water and pastures. Today, many Tuareg people live a settled life. The Tuareg are Muslims and have a distinctive language with its own alphabet. There are around five million Tuareg people.

WODAABE COURTSHIP RITUALS

The Wodaabe nomadic people of Niger have a unique ritual for finding a marriage partner. Once a year, the young men dress up and parade in front of the women. The men try to outshine one another and attract the females by wearing makeup called *yaake*, making strange faces, and performing strenuous dances called *gerewol*. Each woman chooses the man she finds the most attractive.

DINKA CATTLE HERDERS

The Dinka people of southern Sudan grow crops and raise herds of animals, especially cattle. The cattle supply milk and meat, and their urine is used as an antiseptic. At dusk, families and their animals gather around fires made from cow dung. The smoke protects the people from insects. Ash from the dung fires can be rubbed onto the skin to repel insects. Ash is also used for makeup and toothpaste. It is the job of the young men to take care of the cattle, protecting them from predators and raids by other tribes. Cattle are called into their evening compounds by the beating of a drum. They recognize the beat played by their owner and respond to the individual song. Cattle are selected for the size of their horns and represent a Dinka family's wealth.

LIFE & TRADITION

Africa today is a fascinating mix of old and new. In many parts of the continent, there are beautiful modern cities. However, there are also many traditional villages, where villagers still live more or less exactly as they did five hundred years ago. Tribesmen still live as part of immense "families" that collectively own the land. They are a living record of the way things were. In many African villages, the community as a whole raises the children. Homes are built largely identically and are made from the materials around them. Even today, homes in an African village might be built of thick mud walls decorated with intricate designs.

THE AMHARA OF ETHIOPIA

The Amhara people of the central highlands of Ethiopia are Semitic and have more in common with Arab countries than they do with Africa. The Amhara adopted Christianity more than 1,700 years ago. In Lalibela, Ethiopia, they carved churches out of the solid rock of the hillside. The Amhara eat *teff*, a grain not grown by any other culture. They make it into big pancakes.

THE ZULU

In the early 1800s, the Zulu became the mightiest military force in southern Africa. Today, almost eight million Zulu live in the countryside of Kwa-Zulu Natal, South Africa. Many Zulu men are forced to make a living working in coal mines hundreds of miles from their homes and families. Believing that evil spirits cause bad luck and disease, Zulu consult *isangomas*, specially trained healers who diagnose illnesses and their causes. The problems are then treated with traditional Zulu medicines made by an *inyanga*. Many Zulu women are skilled in making craft items from beads. If a woman wants to start a relationship with a man, she may send a message to him through her beaded jewelry.

MASAI CATTLE HERDERS

The Masai cattle herders live a semi-nomadic life in the Great Rift Valley of southern Kenya and northern Tanzania. Masai men are grouped into an age group with their peers. They remain with this group for all the stages of their lives, doing different work during each stage. Masai women take care of the children, collect firewood and water, grow vegetables, and even build the family's home. Because it is high in protein, cattle blood is extracted from a vein in a cow's neck and given to people suffering from a variety of illnesses. During ceremonies, the *moran* (young warriors) perform rhythmic jumps that they continue for hours.

THE ASHANTI PEOPLE OF GHANA

The Ashanti people live in southern Ghana. Arts and crafts are traditionally very important within their culture. Craftworkers carve wooden stools with images that reflect the owners' personalities. Many people in Ghana are buried in coffins specially carved into shapes that are specific to their lives, such as musical instruments or animals if they were farmers. Ashanti weavers produce elaborately patterned cloth called *kente*. A special type of *kente* cloth is made for and worn only by the Asasnehene, the Ashanti king.

SOUTH AFRICAN TOWNSHIP LIFE

In South Africa, people from all over the country have moved to the cities looking for work. They live in townships, which are shanty towns on the edges of cities. People build their own houses from whatever materials they can find, and often do not have running water, sanitation, or electricity. Many people are unable to find work or have low-paid temporary jobs. The mix of people from across the country can make a township a poor, yet vibrant, place. Township people enjoy a wide range of exciting music.

DID YOU KNOW?

Which country sent the most explorers to Africa?

The explorers of Africa came from all over the continent of Europe. However, it was the small country of Scotland that produced more explorers than any other. The list of Scottish explorers includes Mungo Park, David Livingstone, Joseph Thomson, Hugh Clapperton, and Verney Lovett Cameron. It is difficult to find a reason why Scottish explorers outnumbered all others. It is certainly true that Scottish people traveled all over the world in the 1800s to start a new life in a new land. Many modern Americans and Australians can trace their family line back to Scotland.

How Stanley carried his boat, the *Lady Alice*, overland?

Both Livingstone and Stanley relied on boats to explore the interior of Africa. However, there were many times when they had to be carried because the river was too shallow or rocky, or there was a waterfall. Stanley made the job easier by having his boat divided into eight sections. Each section was light enough to be carried by two African porters and could easily be fastened together again.

Why Europeans were so fascinated by the African city of Timbuktu?

Many of the European explorers who came to Africa did so in order to enter the Malian city of Timbuktu. Founded in the 1000s, it became a major center of Muslim learning and culture in the 1400s. One of the world's first universities was established here. Like the holy city of Mecca, it was out of bounds to non-Muslims so, for Europeans, it represented the mystery of Muslim culture. If Timbuktu could be understood, then so might the rest of the Muslim world.

Who the first white person to see a gorilla was?

The American explorer, Paul de Chaillu, returned home from Africa in 1859 with the first report of a gorilla sighting by a white person. He wrote: "Nearly six feet high, with immense body, huge chest, and great muscular arms, with fiercely glaring large deep gray eyes and a hellish expression of face, which seemed to me like some nightmare vision." His description did much to damage the reputation of this gentle animal and gave rise to films like *King Kong*.

What a diamond is?

A diamond is a mineral that is made of pure, natural carbon. The atoms are packed closely together in cube shapes, making it the hardest substance in the world. The largest diamond was found in South Africa in 1902 and was called the Cullinan diamond. It weighed over 2 lbs. (1kg) and was cut up to produce several gemstones for the British crown jewels. This includes the "Star of Africa," the largest cut diamond in the world today.

How much of Africa's rainforest has been destroyed?
Almost 90 percent of the rainforest in West Africa has been destroyed. 90 percent of the rainforest on the African island of Madagascar has been destroyed. Around 80 percent of the animal species found on Madagascar live only on this island and nowhere else on Earth (other than in zoo populations).

Which African country was the first to protect the environment?
Namibia was the first country in the world to include protecting the environment in its constitution. Around 14 percent of Namibia is now protected, including the entire Namib Desert coast.

Which country was the first to grow coffee?
It is believed that the first place in the world to cultivate coffee was Ethiopia. It was grown in the Kefa region of Ethiopia around 1,000 years ago.

How Islam spread within Africa?
In Africa most people followed their own religion and their own customs. However, the part of Africa that lay around the Sahara Desert was dominated by Islam. It was introduced into Africa from two directions. Just south of the Sahara is an area known as the Sahel. For centuries people in the Sahel crossed the Sahara to trade with the Mediterranean. When Islam spread across North Africa in the 600s and 700s, Islam found its way across the desert with the traders. On the east African coast Islam arrived with Arab merchants who sailed down much of the east African coastline.

That apartheid ended in 1994?
Apartheid comes from the Afrikaans word for "apartness." It was a policy of keeping people of different races separate and unequal in a society. Under apartheid in South Africa, black people had less freedom, and power than white people. It was enforced by white minority governments in South Africa from 1948 to 1994.

How much the European explorers were involved in slavery?
From the 1440s the Portuguese used their expeditions along the West African coast to capture people and to take them back to Portugal to sell as slaves. Europeans felt that slavery was justified because the people they had captured were not Christians. Once they became slaves then they could become Christians. Africans began to fight back once they realized why the Europeans were there. Portuguese traders soon realized that it would be easier to buy slaves from traders in the Benin.

That the Zulus write messages in beads?
Many Zulu women are skilled in making craft items from beads. If a woman wants to have a relationship with a man, she may send a subtle message to him through her beaded jewelry.

That the Sahara was not always a desert?
Ancient rock paintings show that 8,000 years ago the Sahara Desert was a lush green place that was home to many wild animals.

GLOSSARY

abolish To get rid of or do away with.

amphitheater An oval or round building with seats rising in rows from an open, central area. Amphitheaters are used for sports and other public events.

apartheid A policy of keeping people of different races separate and unequal in a society.

aristocracy A class of peole who have a high social position because of the family they are born into. Members of the aristocracy are usually richer and have more privileges than other members of society.

aristocrat A member of the aristocracy.

botanist A person who studies the science of plants.

caravan A band of people traveling together.

cholera A disease marked by severe vomiting and diarrhea that is often fatal.

Christian A person who believes in the divine nature of Jesus Christ and follows his words and teachings.

Christianity A religion based on the teachings of Jesus Christ.

civilization The culture and way of life of a people, nation, or period regarded as a stage in the development of organized society.

colony A place where a group of people come to settle which is under the control of their home country.

commission An instruction, command, or duty given to a person or group of people.

community A group of people who live close together or have shared interests.

conquest Something gained by conquering, such as land or riches.

crusade A war or campaign that is religiously motivated.

democracy A form of government in which power rests with the people, either directly or through elected representatives.

democratic Believing that all people should be treated as equals.

desert A very dry, sandy area with few or no plants growing in it.

developed country A country with a highly organized economy.

diplomat A person whose job is to handle relations with the governments of other countries.

ebony A hard, black wood.

economic Related to the production, distribution, and consumption of goods and services.

equator An imaginary line that circles the Earth, drawn equal distance from the north and south poles.

ethnic Of or relating to a group of people with its own language, history, or culture.

export To send to another country to sell.

extinct No longer existing.

fertile Producing or able to produce farm crops or other plant life.

fortify To give more strength, resistance, or energy to; to reinforce

geologist A person who studies geology.

geology The study of the physical structure of earth and how it has changed over time.

hostile Feeling or showing dislike.

incense A substance that has a pleasant smell when burned.

interior The part of a country that is away from the coast or borders with other countries.

Islam The religion of the Muslims which was founded by Muhammad.

Islamic Of or related to the Muslim religion.

ivory The hard, white material that forms the tusks of elephants and other animals.

journalist The activity or profession of writing for newspapers or magazines.

kingdom A country that is ruled by a king or queen.

Koran The sacred book of Islam that is the basis of Muslim religion.

latitude The distance between the equator and a point north or south on the earth's surface. This distance is measured in degrees.

magnet An object that has the power to pull items made of iron toward itself.

magnetic Having the properties of a magnet.

massacre The killing of a large number of people or animals in a cruel and violent manner.

Mediterranean Sea A large body of water connected to the Atlantic Ocean. It is bordered by Europe to the north, Asia to the east, and Africa to the south.

missionary A person who is sent by a church or religious order to a foreign country to teach, convert, heal, or serve.

Muslim A person who follows the religion of Islam.

mutiny Open disobeying or fighting against the leaders in charge.

myrrh A fragrant gum resin obtained from certain trees, used in perfumes, medicines, and incense.

navigation The act of setting a course for or controlling a ship.

nomad A member of a group or tribe that has no fixed home and moves from place to place.

notorious Famous or well known, typically for something bad.

pastures A piece of land on which animals are put to

plantation A large farm or estate used for growing rubber, cotton, or other crops to sell.

rain forest A dense evergreen forest, mostly found in a tropical area, that receives a large amount of rain all year long.

ritual A set of actions always done in the same way.

savanna A flat plain covered with grass and few trees.

slash-and-burn Cutting a sweeping patch of trees and using fire to reduce and recycle the nutrients contained in them.

slave A person who is owned by and forced to work for another with no pay or rights.

slave trade The capturing, transporting, buying,

and selling of people as slaves.

species A group of living things that can mate with one another but not with those of other groups.

summit The highest part of a hill or mountain.

terrain Land or ground.

trade The act of exchanging or buying and selling goods.

trek To travel or make one's way slowly and with difficulty.

tributary A river or stream that flows into a larger river or stream, or into a lake.

urban Of or having to do with a city or town.

workhouse A public place in which the poor received board and lodging in return for work.

yellow fever A disease passed on by mosquitoes, which affects the liver and kidneys. It causes fever and jaundice (yellowing of the skin and eyes). It is often fatal.

FURTHER READING & WEBSITES

BOOKS

Atlas of Exploration
Andrew Kerr and Francois Naude
(Dorling Kindersley Publications, 2008)

David Livingstone (Great Explorers)
Frances Freedman (Gareth Stevens, 2001)

David Livingstone: African Explorer (Sower Series)
John Tiner (Mott Media, 1997)

*David Livingstone: Africa's Trailblazer
(Christian Heroes: Then & Now)*
Janet Benge and Geoff Benge
(YWAM Publishing, 1999)

*David Livingstone: Deep in the Heart of Africa
(Great Explorations)*
Steven Otfinoski (Benchmark Books, 2006)

Explorer (DK Eyewitness Books)
Rupert Matthews (DK Children, 2005)

Explorers and Exploration
Steadwell Books and Lara Rice Bergen
(Heinemann Library, 2001)

Life In Ancient Africa (Peoples of the Ancient World)
Hazel Richardson
(Crabtree Publishing Company, 2005)

*New York Public Library Amazing Explorers:
A Book of Answers for Kids*
Brendan January (Wiley, 2001)

*Stanley and Livingstone and the Exploration of Africa
in World History*
Richard Worth (Enslow Publishers, 2000)

West Africa (Exploration and Discovery)
Stephen Currie (Lucent Books, 2004)

The World of Exploration
Philip Wilkinson (Kingfisher, 2006)

*Tools of Navigation: A Kid's Guide to the History and
Science of Finding Your Way (Tools of Discovery)*
Rachel Dickinson (Nomad Press, 2005)

WEBSITES

http://academickids.com/encyclopedia/index.php/
David_Livingstone
*An encyclopedic biography of David Livingstone
with great cross-referencing to subjects related
to his voyages.*

http://academickids.com/encyclopedia/index.php/
Henry_Morton_Stanley
*An encyclopedic biography of Henry Morton Stanley
with great cross-referencing to subjects related to
his voyages.*

www.kidport.com/REFLIB/UsaHistory/Explorers/
Explorers.htm
*Information on early explorers, including Christopher
Columbus.*

www.kidskonnect.com/subject-index/16-history/
265-explorers.html
A gateway to sites about the different explorers.

ww2.mariner.org/exploration/index.php
*A useful website from The Mariners' Museum, Virginia
which looks at exploration through the ages. Includes
information on the explorers, ships, tools of
navigation, and voyages.*

www.royalafricansociety.org/index.php?option=com_
content&task=view&id=169&Itemid=165
*The Royal African Society website, U.K., which
contains interesting information about Mary Kingsley.*

INDEX

ACKNOWLEDGMENTS

The publishers would like to thank: Graham Rich, Neil Grant, Jan Alvey, and Elizabeth Wiggans for their assistance, and David Hobbs for his map of Africa. Picture research by Image Select.

Picture Credits: t=top, b=bottom, c=center, l=left, r=right, OFC=outside front cover
AKG: 1, 6bl, 8bl, 8/9c, 16/17t, 18cl, 20/21c, 23tr, 24/25t, 26/27t, 32tl, 32/33t, 32/33b, 34c, 42/43c, 43b. Ann Ronan @ Image Select: 7c, 12bl, 16cb, 24tl, 24bl, 25tr, 25b, 27tr, 28/29t, 29cb, 31br, 32cl, 34/35c. Ann Ronan Picture Library: 16/17b, 19cr, 21bl. Associated Press: 37c. Bridgeman Art Library: 3b, 10bl, 16bl, 22br, 22/23c, 28cb, 28/29 (main pic), 28/29b, 30/31b, 33br, 46, 48. C.F.C.L/Image Select: 5ct, 31tr. Chris Johns/National Geographic Picture Collection: 18/19t. Colourific!: 18/19 (main pic), 36bl. Corbis: 38–39bc, 39r, 40b. e.t.archive: 34bl. Fotomas; 19cl, 23br, 26tl, 29c, 31c. Giraudon: 13br, 10r, 11ct, 16bl, 17r, 20bl, 20ct, 35c. Hulton Getty: 17c, 18c, 21tr, 28l, 32cl, 37br. Image Select: 11br, 13tr, 24br, 35br, 43t. Images of Africa Photobank: 37tr. Institute Amatller D'art Hispanic (Spain): 14tl. Mary Evans Picture Library: 8c, 11tl, 30/31t. Mary Rose Trust: 12tl. NHPA: 6/7t. © Patrick Lorette-Giraudon, Giraudon photographie: 35c. Pix: 4bl, 5b, 8t, 33tr, 45. Planet Earth Pictures: 4tl, 6/7b, 10tl, 14–15, 22/23b, 29tr. Rex Features:36/37c. Shutterstock: OFC. South African Library: 30tl. Spectrum Colour Library: 14–15ct. Telegraph Colour Library: 4tl, 5cb, 18tl. Werner Forman Archive: 6/7c, 42b, 44b.